# American
# Contemporary
# Houses

# American Contemporary Houses

Telleri

# THE ART OF THE HABITAT

Series directed by Olivier Boissière

*Front cover*
A house in Chicago,
Illinois. Architect:
Krueck & Sexton.

*Back cover*
A house in Chicago,
Illinois. Architect:
Krueck & Sexton.

*Preceding page*
A house in San Diego,
California. Architect:
Jeanne McCallum.

Publisher editor: Jean-François Gonthier
Art director: Bruno Leprince
Cover design: Daniel Guerrier
Editing staff: Hortense Lyon, Charles Bilas, Véronique Donnat
Translation: Rubye Monet, Unity Woodman
Assistant to the publisher: Sophie-Charlotte Legendre
Correction and revision: Françoise Derray
Composition: Graffic, Paris
Filmsetting: Compo Rive Gauche, Paris
Lithography: ARCO Editorial, Barcelone

This edition copyright © TELLERI, PARIS 1998
All illustrations copyright © ARCO Editorial except for the front and back covers © TELLERI
ISBN : 2-7450-0021-7
Printed in the European Community

TELLERI - 30, rue de Charonne - F-75011 Paris

# Contents

# Introduction

The American home has grown out of a tradition now officially over two hundred years old, a tradition from which a few well-ingrained ideas persist in collective memory: the log cabin of the pioneers, Thomas Jefferson's neo-Palladian mansion, the plantation of Scarlett O'Hara, the California bungalow and the aristocratic Victorian house, in its East and West Coast versions. Then came the great Frank Lloyd Wright to add his imprint, a mark still felt today, and finally the wave of immigrants, of different schools and tendencies, who introduced various touches of European modernism.

The American house is modern by nature. It is distinguished from its European counterpart by certain specific features: the garage that is given pride of place at the front of the house, not surprising in a society so dominated by the automobile; the oversized kitchen which, paradoxically, often lacks the conviviality of the European version; the living areas that extend outward toward the garden; and the relaxed interpenetration of interior and exterior space.

Each great area of the American continent has its own climate, culture and way of life, giving rise to particular architectural forms. The East Coast lifestyle differs from that of the Middle West. The Deep South, the Southwest and the Pacific Coast have their specificities which, far from creating a homogeneous American dwelling, have deepened and accentuated the differences of style and character. In addition, Americans, who pride themselves on their "rugged individualism," have made their homes an expression of their personality, their social status and even of their imagination or their wildest fantasy.

With a quiet boldness born of self-confidence, American architecture over the past two decades has developed an identity that is varied and unabashedly eclectic. Its practitioners today include some of the first-rate architects in the world, which has, of course, greatly contributed to its international renown. This in turn has given rise to a growing number of clients whose ambitions and aspirations have spurred the imagination and creativity of the architects and contributed to the astonishing liberty of form that is well-attested by the houses presented in this book.

A house in Santa Monica, California.
Architect : Ray Kappe

*Ross S. Anderson*

# A house in Napa Valley, California

The house seems to have sprung up from the rocky soil. With its large picture window held between two protruding "cheeks," it opens out onto the landscape.

*Opposite page*
The south facade and the swimming pool viewed at dusk. The pool's red terra cotta border and the beige breeze blocks play off each other beautifully.

**P**erched on top of a hill overlooking the Napa Valley, amidst an almost Mediterranean vegetation, this odd construction juts out against the stark blue California sky. It evokes both a fairy tale castle – a faraway retreat for some evil witch escaped from Disneyland – and the body of a 1950's Reflex camera.

Located near the town of Rutherford, this house of no more than 150 square meters (1,600 square feet), was built as a main residence. Its design combines straightforward and traditional materials to achieve both dramatic tension and even a certain mischievousness. Designed by architect Ross S. Anderson, it was completed in 1989.

Its wooden construction would be in perfect keeping with the local customs if its main body was not held in the grips of two cement blocks. This unique layout splits the house into two distinct sections.

The main entrance is located on the back facade – on the north side – sheltered by a wooden pergola resting on six cement pillars around which a nervous wisteria twists and turns. A picturesque roof in the shape of a policeman's hat juts out beyond the wall. Nestled in the roof and pointing its arrow to the sky is a mullion window raised by a triangular piece of glass. The rest of the facade is closed and uniform.

A side view of the house from the southeast highlights the construction's perfect integration with the California landscape.

*Opposite page*
The long narrow pool extends beyond the natural drop of the terrain, its expressive outline standing out against a hazy backdrop.

On the opposite end – on the southern side – the building opens outward with its large square window mounted between the two concrete outer portions of the ground floor. Upstairs, a long strip of windows under the overhang of the roof adds a touch of modernity to a vocabulary based on traditional construction techniques and materials. As though under pressure from the tight hold of the building's lateral jaws, the upstairs literally pushes outwards from the box of Sequoia forming its base.

Four steps lead down to a narrow swimming pool set into the extension of the house, aligned with the view of a small lake lower down in the valley. This alignment sets the pool off slightly to the east, producing a striking effect of slippage. Swimmers can see the lake from the border of the pool through the branches of age-old oak trees. The relatively small slope under the edifice is suddenly accentuated when it drops below the pool, creating a raise of some 2 meters (6 feet) high and amplifying the expressionist feel to the ensemble.

The facing of the walls on the ground floor is rough and mostly light colored with Sequoia paneling for the central part and cement breeze blocks for the two extensions. This sets up a contrast with the darker varnishing upstairs and the mat gray of the lead roof, soon to take on the soft hues of green with oxidation.

It should be noted that the particular shape of this building is a studied response to a very real fire danger. This explains the concrete and water on the southern facade, the swimming pool serving as an emergency reservoir. With its

The door from the
sitting room fireplace
leading directly to the
pool on the south
facade.

The block containing
the fireplace with its
metal chimney jutting
forward on the west
facade. The breeze
blocks, in equal halves
on either side of the
main body of the
house, start in line with
the edge of the roof.

The compact kitchen has wooden paneling and hardwood floors, present throughout the house. A narrow staircase, tucked behind it, leads to the upstairs bedrooms.
Three varieties of wood used for the paneling, furniture and floors create a delicate harmony, with accents of white for the ceiling, door and window frames.

The living room's large picture window frames the bucolic view of the wine country. Notice the subtle echo between the reflection on the surface of the pool and that of the glass coffee table.

large overhang, the metal roof also protects the house from embers blown by the wind. The walls of the basement are 2 x 15 centimeters (2 x 6 inches) thick and upstairs, 2 x 10 centimeters (2 x 4 inches); the perimeter is finished with a clear fireproof varnish to protect the wood.

The main entry leads directly into the living/dining room, lit up by its large picture window and the view extending beyond the still surface of the pool to the valley and vineyards below. Two couches, one against the wall and the other opposite a glass table, form the principal furnishings. The inevitable corner of the fireplace is tucked into one of the concrete cubes. The paneled kitchen with its three pale green chairs gives out directly onto the living room. In the second concrete cube, on the first floor, is a storage room, a sauna and an outdoor shower next to the swimming pool.

Upstairs, accessed by a staircase following the rear wall, are two sunny bedrooms and their small adjoining bathroom. In the same spirit as the rest of the house, the furnishing is kept to a minimum. The bedrooms give out onto terraces with stunning views over the valley, this time from an even higher elevation.

Finally, in the attic nestled under the framework of the roof, a futon, soft cushions scattered here and there, a pair of bedside tables and a chair turn this vast space into a bedroom. The triangular window and the intertwining honey-colored beams complete the picture.

As we have seen, this is an altogether light and simple house, an invitation to fully enjoy the peace and rest of the spectacular California sunsets. □

The bedrooms upstairs are lined in sequoia
with built-in beds and drawers. The beds take
up the shaft formed by the living room window
on the ground floor.

*Opposite page*
Bathed in a golden light reflecting off the
rafters, another blissful bedroom.

The materials making up the fireplace corner
are the same rough breeze blocks and terra
cotta as on the exterior. The lighting from its
small opening in the walls and ceiling adds its
warmth to this intimate nook.

# A house in Albuquerque, New Mexico

View of the main
entrance. The
construction seems to
have emerged out of
the rock itself to cast
its unusual shapes –
mineral, plant and
animal – against the
blue sky.

*Opposite page*
Bart prince excels in
combining different
shapes, materials,
textures and colors.
The red ocher walls
recall indigenous clay
constructions.

In this vast land of contrasts, the unexpected still springs forth, either from its fervent nature or from the inventiveness of its inhabitants.

Here in New Mexico, at the edge of the Rockies on an arid plateau nestled at the foot of a steep rock face, a giant mushroom rises out of the sand and rocks. In this inhospitable soil, it appears to have shot up out of nowhere, as though sown by some mysterious creator.

This is in fact a secondary residence designed by the high-profile architect Bart Prince for his parents Brad and June. Their dream was to live in a house open to the four winds with views as far as the eye can see. Not only did their talented son grant their wish, he did so beyond their greatest expectations.

The construction sits on over an acre formed by a rocky bed at the foot of the Sandia Crest to the far north-east of Albuquerque. Looking west, the eye can see over a stretch of almost 150 kilometers as far as the Rio Grande. The eastern chain of mountains is also visible, as well as the Indian reservations to the north.

It is difficult to describe with accuracy such a complex "machine" as this. However, the house can be broken down

Viewed at dusk, the outline of this original construction blends in perfectly with the landscape of New Mexico.

Floor plan of the main living area on the ground floor also showing the general layout of the building.

1. Living room
2. Kitchen
3. Toilet
4. Bedroom
5. Bathroom
6. Bedroom
7. Bedroom
8. Passage
9. Sitting room

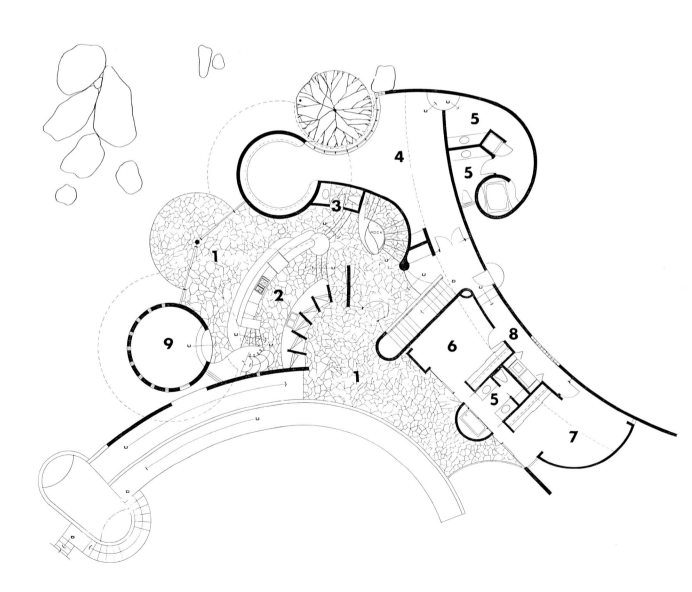

Distinct against the backdrop of a stunning mountain range, three "mushrooms" with curious metal tentacles fan out toward the valley of the Rio Grande.

Indoors, "parasols" spread out around a central metallic mast.

Set into the curve of the surrounding wall, the windows participate in the dialogue between transparency and opacity, between the interior and the natural setting.

*Opposite page*
The central platform overlooks the kitchen tucked in below. The large windows end in a the stone wall with steps and varied openings. Above, the massive steel beams support the roof and the wooden "parasols" to which they are attached.

into three juxtaposed and overlapping cylinders that emerge out of its rocky stand to form a wide fan, open to the west onto the valley of the Rio Grande.

To adapt his construction to the topography and to hide the garages in the back, Prince built double stone walls to curve around the edifice. Where they break down into steps, they are reminiscent of some ancient ruin. The cylinders enclose the least "formal" areas, while the private bedrooms are located in another lateral wing.

The living room is a large volume on more than one level that includes the kitchen, dining room, sitting room and even a smoking room, along with various other areas for family life in what resembles a glass-covered gallery. Overhead, a series of robust steel rods fan out from the central kitchen toward the glass periphery. Suspended from these rods are three large disks made up of concentric wooden beams and joined by metal plates. They form both the ceiling and the roof of the structure.

The dining room takes up a raised circular platform underneath one of these "parasols," some 9 meters (28 feet) in diameter, with a shaft of light passing through its center. Set symmetrically on the other side, another cylinder holds a cozy sitting room, curled around a large stone fireplace. Between these two, a third cylinder, almost entirely made of glass, forms a verandah ideally angled for taking in the view. Silvery quartz flagstones line all the floors, including those of the terraces.

One accesses the lateral wing through a small hallway that leads to an impressive suite with master bedroom, bathroom and a spacious closet. The centerpiece of the room is a large circular window built around an old weeping willow, a tree Prince wanted to keep at all costs. Through the other side of the hallway, after the stairs to the garage, are two guest rooms, joined by a corridor and a bathroom. Their windows give out onto the extension of the entrance terrace, accessible on the south facade along a curved ramp.

The long stone wall that borders this northern wing provides a protective screen against the often violent winter storms and ensures the privacy of these rooms. The other surrounding walls are clad in red stucco, reminiscent of the clay constructions still found on Indian reservations in the neighborhood.

Bart Prince draws his inspiration from his mentor Bruce Goff with whom he collaborated on many projects. He has been equally inspired by Frank Lloyd Wright and even Gaudí – a true revelation in his youth.

In front of the glass entrance door, a carpet from a distant land adds a welcoming touch.

*Opposite page*
In the kitchen, all the furnishings, including the built-in curved counter tops in varying heights, set the tone and add warmth to the interior decoration.

This is the dining area where, to the left, one can see the verandah and the "organic" stone fireplace of the sitting room – a fireplace that would have appealed to Gaudí.

*Opposite page*
From the staircase leading to the sitting room, one can clearly see the overlap of the three wooden "parasols" and the circular opening in the center of the two outer ones.

Gifted with an exceptional feel for nature – a characteristic trait of the American school – he has once again created a strong and profoundly original work that stands out from its neighboring pale archetypes, having taken up the challenge to build where no one has ventured to build before. □

# A house in Santa Monica, California

**B**uilt amid the trees on the flank of a mountain, this house is solidly anchored to the ground by a vertically-placed concrete parallelepiped, from which extend on either side at various levels, balconies and terraces. These horizontal extensions or projections form zones of expansion at each level and provide unique views over Rustic Canyon, where this property is situated. One reaches the house from the road below by a driveway up to the front gate.

This structure of concrete, glass and steel announces clearly the modernism to which California architect Ray Kappe is unquestionably the heir.

The entrance facade on the north is monumental, with the massive bearing of a fortress. Five slit windows adorn a rampart of bare concrete, whose only decoration is a uniform grid pattern that echoes the thick glass blocks on the west front. This vertical block with its terraces rising up to the summit exudes a strong sculptural power.

All the attributes of modernism are here, in the materials used as well as in the geometry of the volumes. However, Ray Kappe's building holds some surprises in store - you need only walk around it to find them. On the other side of the concrete wall that cuts the building in two from west to east, the south of the house, facing the mountains, is

This fortress made of concrete, glass and steel adapts the vocabulary of modernism to the demands of ecology. The rounded forms, the colors and materials of the gateway give an exact prefiguration of what is to follow.

The entrance facade is a complex
assemblage of overlapping
geometric forms with rounded
edges. Despite the massive
appearance, it finds a perfect
equilibrium between horizontals
and verticals.

*Opposite page*
A wall running west to east cuts
the building in two and masks the
wall of glass that forms the back
of the house, facing the
mountains.

transparent, in complete contrast with the opacity of the front. The metal structure that arches downward from roof to ground forms an immense glass dome. Here the architect is responding, with a modernism tempered by ecology, to present preoccupations of California architecture, particularly in tune with the environment. Solar energy obtained via the glass roof is stored, then redistributed during the cool hours of night. The entire house is equipped with a sophisticated system of autoregulation of temperature, thanks to captors of atmospheric variations.

The spacious inner areas are lit from above by the glass roof. The space is ordered around the central staircase, partly covered by a concrete sheath. This reddish-brown metallic structure climbs gracefully to the top of the building, to a terrace that dominates the whole surrounding landscape.

The interior decoration is elegant and sober. Concrete walls, floors either tiled or carpeted, ceiling covered with fine wooden slats, and simple, comfortable furniture form a harmony in white, gray and beige, set off by occasional touches of black or dark brown. The living room, kitchen and dining room fill a large space, open but clearly delimited so as to provide each area with a different light and atmosphere.

On the top floor, the bedroom has a place of choice under the glass roof, suspended between the sky and the forest canopy. Concrete, glass and steel - what could be simpler? And the metal bed posed in the middle of the room has no need to burden itself with any decoration - the spectacle beyond the glass is sufficient. □

The interior volumes follow an open
plan, spacious and fluid with many
differences in level.

*Opposite page*
With the light streaming in from above,
stairs and passageways stand out like
bits of calligraphy against
the concrete walls.

The kitchen, like the
dining room, occupies
the end of one of the
horizontal "arms",
completely open onto
the outside.

*Fay Jones*

# A house in Evergreen, Colorado

The house marked by
the dynamic tension in
its play of contrasts:
horizontals, verticals
and oblique angles;
material and
emptiness; white walls
and wooden surfaces;
glass and stone.

*Opposite page*
Donning the
appearance of an eagle
about to take flight, the
house has large
extensions of the roof
to protect the facades
from heavy weather.

**V**iewed from a certain angle, this building with the taught lines of its immense roof, evokes a huge bird of prey momentarily perched on a rocky promontory dominating the valley below.

In choosing this particular shape, the well-known architect Fay Jones was responding as much to geographical and climatic conditions as to his client's request to combine a studio and home under the same roof.

Located near Evergreen, Colorado, at an altitude of 2,200 meters (7,000 feet) the terrain covers some five acres in the rugged peaks and thick forests of the Rocky Mountains. The house overlooks a terraced garden on one side, while on the other, the view encompasses a more distant and wild landscape.

The floor plan of this two-storey construction involves a complex geometrical form evoking an "X" inscribed within a diamond. The house has its main entry to the east (on the garden side) preceded by an open courtyard. Once inside, a hallway connects the main areas of the ground floor where a large living room in the center extends, on its south end, into

On the western facade, a large bow-window gives out onto a raised
stone terrace. Upstairs, the studio's wooden balcony provides
additional shade for the windows on the ground floor.

*Opposite page*
The main door on the east side, preceded by a paved entranceway,
occupies the center of a glass expanse taking up the full facade.
Through the window, crossed by the railings of the studio balcony, one
can see the majestic view stretching all the way to the Rocky
Mountains to the west.

The entrance porch and
details of the angular
wooden structure
supporting the upstairs
balcony.

*Opposite page*
The dining room with its
striking unity of design,
from the framework of the
beams, the mezzanine's
balustrade to the furniture
and light fixtures.

an adjacent kitchen. Facing the entrance is a large terrace with a view to the west, while to the north are two bedrooms separated by a common bathroom. Almost all of these rooms have generously high ceilings. In the hallway to the right of the door, a spiral staircase leads upstairs.

Here we have an immense working studio and adjoining storage space that encircles the open center of the living room. The studio has large glass windows that open out onto two balconies facing east and west. Light is thus plentiful, the *sine qua non* of all pictorial creation.

The two square towers, on the south and the north of the hearth cavity, rise up from this floor. On a structural level, these two vertical elements, held in place by the principal cross-shaped rafters, ensure a brace against the strong cross winds; after all, homes in this area must be designed to withstand heavy snowfalls and often violent winds.

Furthermore, these rafters, like "scissors," provide two pairs of tall windows on either side of the rooftree, bringing in abundant natural light to the studio. More diffuse light is then filtered down through the empty center to the living room where it softens the more concentrated light from the windows on the facade.

In order to guard against too much sunlight and heat, the architect has designed the roofs to overhang the facades and balconies, simultaneously reducing the risk of wind gusts on the large windows. The roofs and walls are also well insulated, again in response to climatic conditions. Likewise, all the windows, skylights and glass walls have double glazing. Air conditioning is not needed thanks to the natural airflow that this design affords, an electrical heating system under the floors making for all-around comfort.

The bulk of the house is built in reinforced concrete, while the outside walls are formed by wooden frames filled in with plaster or expanses of glass. The overall framework is in wood and clad in the same material. Inside, the floors are alternately laid down in flagstones or hardwood; the dividing walls and cupboards have pinewood paneling in gypsum gray.

Fay Jones has instilled a certain harmony throughout. His unifying principle is his variation on the angle, visible in the joining of pillars and beams, down to the last detail of the furniture and lighting. What results is at once a work space and a home, a source of energy and light, a refuge that jealously guards the privacy of its occupants. □

The view from the studio mezzanine reveals the floor's subtle patchwork of such varied materials as stone, wood and the wool of the carpets.

A view across the living room's empty center of the sunny western end of the studio.

*Opposite page*
The living room fireplace and the chimneys built into the south tower with the principal rafters that brace the structure on either side.

The studio mezzanine also gracefully overhangs the bedrooms. The balcony's railings are identical to those on the exterior.

*Opposite page*
The spiral staircase leads to the eastern end of the studio which extends into a terrace beyond a large expanse of windows. The vertical rafters set up an interesting dialogue with the tree trunks beyond.

# A house in Beverly Hills, California

The house, consisting basically of two rectangular blocks, deploys its multi-faceted volumes in the middle of a garden.

**T**he late Frank Israel, the brilliant architect who died before his time, had a singular destiny. As a young man of talent, he studied at the American Academy in Rome, then joined the Lwellyn Davis team of architects and urban planners on what was to be their adventure in Iran. When their work was interrupted by the death of the Shah, Israel returned to New York but, no longer feeling at home in his native city, moved to California.

Faced with the difficulties of getting started in architecture, he began to work in films. In the film world he got his first commissions as an architect and, encouraged by Frank Gehry, returned to his initial vocation. Lucid and modest, Israel saw that there was but a narrow path between the revolutions of Robert Venturi and Frank Gehry. He was, however, able to find his own way – that of a fragmented and sensual architecture, with a composition that was free yet rigorous at the same time, part of a tradition of California modern that owed more to the fantasy of Rudolf Schindler than to Richard Neutra's rigor.

As is often the case in Los Angeles, this project called for nothing more than to enlarge and redesign an ordinary bungalow. The general form of the house consisted of two rectangular parallelepipeds joined together for part of their

The diversity of
volumes and materials
is equaled by the
precision of the lines,
visible in the details of
the front gate, the
design of the roof at
the rear of the house,
or the treatment of the
roofing around the
swimming pool.

An outer wall – the color of the California sky.

In cross-section, one can see the slight difference in the height of the terrain.

length. The only real addition to the initial plan was to place a bathroom in avolume projecting from one of the facades.

From the combination of concrete, steel, brick and wood emerges a complex volume of a visual and tactile richness worthy of the talent of a sculptor. On the facade the galvanized steel resembles a modern variation on shingle siding, while elsewhere, on the roof over the swimming pool, it creates a delicate texture reminiscent of a waffle-iron. Here the plaster plays with light, highlighting the irregularities of its texture. Elsewhere a wooden lining peeps out from under the overhang of a roof. Farther on, red brick exalts a wall of transparent blue: this is the entrance. A gate, framed in the asymmetric harmony of an upside down "L," opens onto the pool, terraces and garden. From the gate, a path leads left toward an area of coolness and leafy shade. After a little way, and a slight difference in height, the shaded passage opens onto a light-filled living room that gently plays with cool harmonies of white, gray and blue, warmed by the blond wood. Contrasting with the entrance axis, the longitudinal axis of the living room is marked out by the assertive lines of its parallel pillars, which guide the eye and the perspective to the glazed front: the spare lines of a tripartite facade surmounted by a roof. On one side of the living room is a separate video room, while the respective space on the other side is occupied by a bedroom.

Frank Israel displayed the same creativity in the design and arrangement of the interior volumes as in the molding of the outer shell. The wealth of his vocabulary is every bit as impressive. Same sense of color, using harmonies of white, gray and blue, same balance in the succession of solids and open space, same sensuality in the combination of textures, from the steel that borders the base of the bed to the wood of the beams. One feels the same freedom in his use of lines: they emphasize the great directional axes or delicately outline the silhouette of a shelf. They can confer a graceful curve to a ceiling and have the power to give steel the softness of fabric, or to follow the geometry of a ceiling-lath to give birth to the canopy of a bed. Frank Israel was a master of line as well as of volume, as much a virtuoso draughtsman as he is a sculptor. □

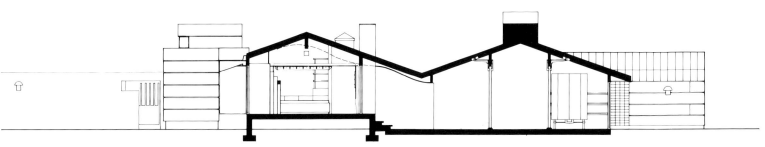

Ground floor

1. Entrance
2. Living room
3. Dining room
4. Kitchen
5. Bedroom
6. Study area
7. Bedroom
8. Bedroom
9. Bathroom
10. Toilet

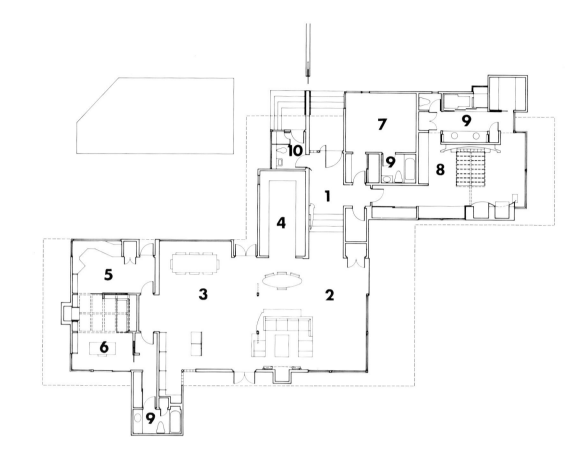

Floor plan and projection showing the relation of the two parallelepipeds, the entrance axis of the house and an additional volume that holds the bathroom.

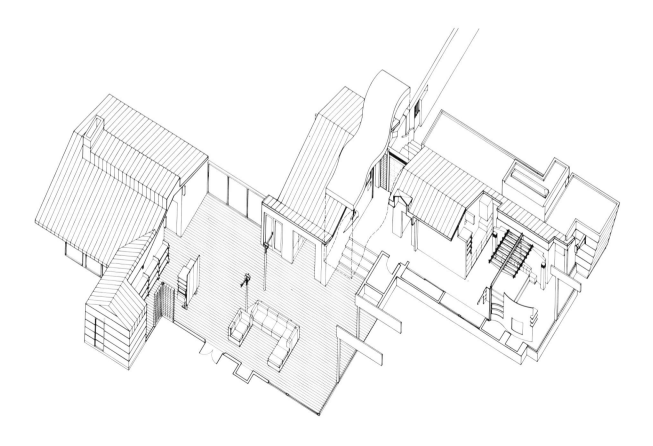

The furniture was
designed by the
architect himself. In the
bedroom, the fireplace
and the hi-fi stand side
by side in the same
curve. In the living
room, a made-to-order
unit holds the records.

Four elongated wooden
figures stand guard in
front of the kitchen.

The living room is
spacious and amply open
to the outside. The
beams and metal pillars
designate the axis of the
room and also serve to
support the lighting
fixtures.

From the hallway,
through the bedroom
and into the living
room, the lines and the
harmonies of blue, gray
and ocher give the
house its internal unity.

# A house in Chicago, Illinois

**C**hicago – the modern city par excellence, the city where the skyscraper was born, where the great Frank Lloyd Wright first practiced, the city that welcomed Mies Van der Rohe when he arrived here as a refugee from Germany and commissioned him to design the campus of the famous IIT, Illinois Institute of Technology, of which he was the longtime head. Was it perhaps a need to exorcise the spirit of the great master? For after his death, here more than elsewhere, architects yielded to the temptations of postmodernism, giving themselves up to the delights of historic pastiche redefined by popular culture.

Both graduates of IIT, Ronald Krueck and Mark Sexton have remained true to the spirit of Mies Van der Rohe and see themselves as being resolutely modern. Situated in a residential district of north Chicago, the Zorn House, which they called the Brick and Glass House, is a discreet homage to Mies Van der Rohe's Berlin period. The house offers the

Unlike the houses that surround it, which all face the street, the Zorn house opens southward on the garden. At night the house shines like an incandescent cage of glass.

56 A house in Chicago, Illinois

A geometry of straight lines
and primary colors. Whether
transparent or opaque, the
facades show their heritage of
neoplasticism.

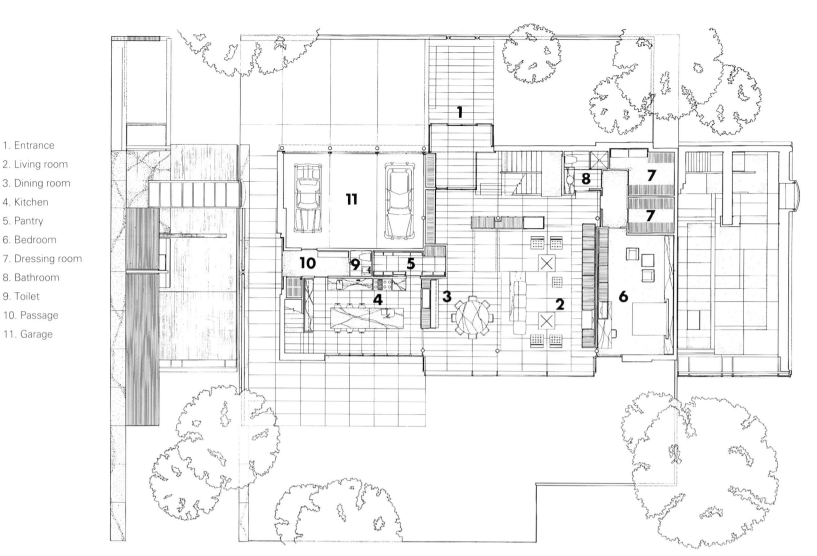

1. Entrance
2. Living room
3. Dining room
4. Kitchen
5. Pantry
6. Bedroom
7. Dressing room
8. Bathroom
9. Toilet
10. Passage
11. Garage

The organization of space, as well as the decoration, are based on the rectangle, as shown in this plan of the ground floor.

*Opposite page*
A touch of brick red brings a hint of warmth into a mineral universe where cool tones dominate.

scope for new variations and marks the desire of Krueck and Sexton to open other horizons to modernity.

The building has the general form of a rectangular parallelepiped placed perpendicular to the adjacent houses. The street side facade is a brick wall split by a large slot extending all the way to the roof and opening the upper storey to light from above. As is common in American cities, it is here that we find the garage, curiously faced with pink stone, and a service entrance masked by a low wall. The front displays a harmonious asymmetry, abstract and rather hermetic. On the garden side the house is generously open by a transparent facade behind a grid of steel and glass. The daily life of the Zorn family unfolds here as on a stage. The layout is traditional, with common rooms on the ground floor and the bedrooms and a library upstairs.

The main entrance gives access, after the vestibule, to an immense living room, mineral in tone as if set in stone. The empty space cut out of the center exposes the spectacle of its geology, its structure and the evolution of its construction. The basic rectangle seems to have been subjected to two forces: one has caused an overlap on the upper floor, where a bedroom and the library invade the

In the bedroom the peaceful lines are an invitation to read or rest in an environment of warm colors.

*Opposite page*
The living room rises dramatically the entire height of the two floors.

volume in the form of mezzanines. Another has projected the living room onto the facade, in the form of a slight protrusion over the garden. For Krueck and Sexton, the succession of volumes serves as a pretext to work the space as they would a plane surface, manipulating surface and colors like an immense canvas in the manner of a neo-plastic painter. But mixed with the primary colors are intermediate tones of violet, gray-green or coral that the members of De Stijl movement would never have accepted. The combined effects of lighting and color instill a touch of unreality into the decor. Fragments of wall float in a state of weightlessness, like metaphors of an aquatic world embedded in the wall. Responding in a sort of counterpoint to the straight lines, a soft mattress and some casually scattered cushions lie on the floor. Krueck and Sexton have made an art of cultivating paradox, of pushing modernity to the limits of mannerism. ☐

# A house in Los Angeles, California

A sculpture garden precedes the house. Like most of the houses in this quarter of Los Angeles, it is pale in color and modest in size, yet it possesses a wonderful spatial quality, visible through the amply transparent facade.

Isozaki was working on a project of the Los Angeles Museum of Contemporary Art when he became acquainted with Teresa Bjornson, a gallery owner and collector of contemporary art. This house was born of that encounter. Situated near Venice Beach, it serves at the same time as a residence, workplace and exhibition venue.

The entrance to the house is preceded by a courtyard paved with slabs of polished concrete. A garden table, a giant cactus plant and a circle of stones assembled by the hand of an artist compose an artificial garden, as dry as the California desert. The facade is its boundary but also its extension, for through the broad glass surface formed by the succession of doors and windows, we can perceive a less arid landscape, covered with blond wood flooring – the exhibition hall, which occupies a vast space at the front of the building.

Through the high window we can glimpse the triangular cutouts, just like the windows facing the front of the house, which create an illusion of a traditional house with a pointed roof. But Isozaki taps the sources of another tradition, modern and minimalist. The front windows look like they could have been designed by the hand of Sol Le Witt. The square is the essential basis of a design based on rigor and

Detail of the north facade.
Doors and windows form a
grill through which we see
the exhibition space that
occupies the entire front of
the house.

*Opposite page*
From inside, a high window
offers an unexpected view
on the works of
Rauschenberg and
Mario Merz.

precision: on the north side it is multiplied to form a grid, on the south, a few isolated squares form an irregular pattern. The general shape of the edifice results from this basic square model, aligned and superimposed seven times. Its imprint, engraved in the concrete of the facade facing the street, is like the memory of the architect's sketch. The flatness of the roof terrace is interrupted by a glass-covered slit that defines two spaces, one for living the other for exhibitions.

Rauschenberg, Mario Merz and Edward Rusha are privileged guests here, their works benefiting from the light that streams in from above and from a space where the laws of gravity seem to have been diluted in a miracle of geometry; the glass panes that resemble butterfly wings at the four corners of the room seem to have the power of levitation. Isozaki here expresses himself in Japanese, with all the dexterity of an origami artist.

The entrance to the living quarters is an exact reproduction of the outer facade, a horizontal band surmounted by a rectangular window flanked a little higher by two glass triangles. Here the areas are smaller and the ambience a subtle mix of refinement and austerity. The dining room, where warm wood tones dominate, has a unique view from the window. The bedroom has the monastic austerity of the Japanese tradition, one small window, a mattress laid on a wooden structure closer to a table than a bedstead, parquet flooring of slim, deep brown boards. The smooth white bathroom is almost surgical. The decoration is reduced to a single motif of parallel bands. Venetian blinds at the corners, neon tubes on the ceiling, the chair backs, the rungs of the ladder leading to the mezzanine even to the oblique frames of the glass panes, punctuate the whiteness of the walls and underscore the edges of the volumes. Soft lighting, a vase, a fruit bowl, together with the architecture, compose a universe of silence and contemplation. □

In the dining room
upstairs and in the
exhibition hall below,
the isoceles triangle,
sometimes as a wall
and sometimes as a
window, adds a very
particular quality to the
overall volume.

In the bedroom the
minimalism of
traditional Japanese
furniture blends well
with the works of
contemporary art.

# A house in Paradise Valley, Arizona

**A**rizona owes its great popularity to its wild desert landscapes and to its warm dry climate, which make it a favorite retirement state.

Nestled between the twin cities of Phoenix and Scottsdale, Paradise Valley is an exclusive little town dominated by the rock-strewn landscape of the Arizona plateau. At the edge of one of these rocky patches, the Zuber family chose to build their house. They could have chosen no architect who was better suited to their aspirations than Antoine Predock, himself a lover of the desert, who has lived since the 1960s in Albuquerque, in the neighboring state of New Mexico.

Antoine Predock has designed a house that is harsh, even forbidding, with a raw and powerful monumentality, not unlike some of the works of Louis Kahn. Like an abstract landscape inspired by the countryside around, it offers a fragmented facade, cut by towers set at acute angles. The marked horizontality of the windows reinforces the impression of contained mass.

All that escapes this solidity is one light metallic structure, like an outstretched arm reaching toward the horizon. Depending on mood and time of day, this metal gangway

Built at the foot of the mountains at the outskirts of Phoenix, this striking construction has all the qualities of a house adapted to desert conditions. With its flat roof, thick walls and bare facades, it composes, with the stark landscape, a startling spectacle.

In the setting sun the
facades take on a reddish
glow from the mountains,
while behind its walls the
house is a cool haven.

*Opposite page*
Above the central patio with
fresh water flowing through
it, the master bedroom
enjoys a double exposure,
north on the surrounding
desert and south toward the
city of Phoenix.

The intricate play of
light and shade – here
in the covered gallery
to the north of the
house. At night, when
the light comes from
within, a walk on this
promenade takes on an
aspect of another
dimension.

The Zuber house is a hospitable home, where art occupies a place of choice, and where guests are welcomed at the family dining table with a stunning view southward toward the city. Facing north, a large picture window looks out over an interior pool and waterfall.

becomes in turn a jutting belvedere, a bridge linking man with the world around him or, more simply, a canopy marking the entrance to the house.

Behind the rampart of concrete and brick, the volumes anchored on the hillside describe an asymmetrical plan, the center of which is a patio cooled by a diamond-shaped pool. Around it are arranged on an east/west axis the bedrooms for family and friends, the living room, dining room and a gallery housing the main part of the master's collections. From north to south the plan follows the irregularities of the slope, descending in three successive degrees to the dining room. Following in the tradition of the Hispano-Moorish palace, Predock makes this hidden place the heart of the house. The running water flows from pool to pool, each in a different geometric shape – a rectangle, a diamond and a circle – marking the entrance to the common areas. This line of water also traces the axis on which is superimposed the upper floor, with the Zuber apartments. The bedroom points its triangular face southward, pierced with two horizontal windows, like two eyes gazing toward the city stretched out below.

Antoine Predock uses the thickness of the walls to direct the view and control the light, sometimes parsimoniously sometimes generously, intentionally framing fragments of nature, like the scenes of a fresco that changes with the rhythm of the seasons. Into rooms with a fragmented geometry, the light enters in great oblique stripes. Elsewhere it forms on blank walls the latticework pattern of an arbor. And when night falls, it creates at the doors of the living room a kind of runway, like a takeoff point for destinations yet unknown. □

In the foreground, the
breakfast nook,
followed by the dining
room and living room
laid out toward the
west.

Sunlight brings out the
golden tones of walls
ranging from soft beige
to deep yellow.

# A house in Albuquerque, New Mexico

This submarine perched on a launching pad, which would look quite at home in a sci-fi film, is in fact the house of an architect. Despite appearances, it is located on an avenue in the heart of a residential quarter of Albuquerque.

**A** native of Albuquerque, Bart Prince belongs to a line of architects who work in the heartland of America, more rural than urban and still carrying the torch of the organic architecture championed by the great Frank Lloyd Wright. Prince was a collaborator and disciple of Bruce Goff, a convinced Wrightian who carried Wright's principles to the limits of expressionism.

The combined house and workshop that Bart Prince has built for himself near the University of Albuquerque comes out of and considerably renews this epic tradition. Its structure evokes, rather than a biological cell, a succession of toothed wheels belonging to some strange machine from a bygone age. It is futuristic and archaic and the same time, both a space age engine and a submarine out of a Jules Verne novel. Thumbing its nose at progress, it seems to disdain the prowess of hi-tech and makes use instead of a very personal assemblage of heterogeneous materials, handled with consummate art. Wooden hull, metal armatures, concrete walls, insulating brick, coverings of cork or ceramic tile, surfaces that are tiled, carpeted, inlaid with mirrors or studded with electric light bulbs, colored mosaics, ringed tubes and crisscrossed pipes, all in a jubilant disorder. Clumps of geraniums hang from its sides like seashells

The floor of the upper level is shaped like the hull of a ship with one side completely open. Two staircases connect with the cylindrical main part of the house. View of staircase roofing, made of steel slats in a fanlike assemblage.

Bart Prince shows his
daring eclecticism and
fertile imagination in
the combination of
materials as well as the
variety of forms.

clinging to the hull of a ship, bouquets of antennas flower here and there to recall that this architecture, which is figurative as well as organic, also takes its sources from Art Nouveau and from the Catalan "modernismo" of Antoni Gaudí.

Around its four cylindrical feet, its points of anchorage on an irregular ground, two spirals of unequal diameter hold staircases that lead to the upper levels. The second level is shared by the guest room and workshop, while the third, all protective roundness carpeted in white, is like a boat sailing into the arms of Morpheus. On the ground floor are the kitchen with its comma-shaped table, the library and the music room. The stairwell is like a dizzying spiral spring that you mount warily, caught in its ascending movement, to the top floor, and arrive, head spinning, on a floor curved like the hull of a ship. On the ceiling, metal beams support glass panes deployed like the wings of some giant bat. Outside, beyond the portholes, lies Marquette Avenue with its neat alignment of prim and proper houses.

Far from the congestion of cities and the trends of fashion, Bart Prince pursues alone an original path to the outer limits of extravagance. In his own way, he bears witness to the jealous individualism of the American citizen. For isn't the pursuit of happiness written into the American Constitution? □

Throughout the house, the dominant figure is the circle. The corridor leading to the upstairs studio forms a spiral, the glass-covered kitchen follows a turning movement, a circular balcony prolongs the corridor leading to the bedrooms, and little round portholes serve as bathroom windows.

A darker space where wood and cork are the dominant materials. This is the architect's studio, where his ideas are born and his plans are first sketched.

*Opposite page*
Upstairs, the corridor on the south is punctuated by fiberglass columns that function as solar captors.

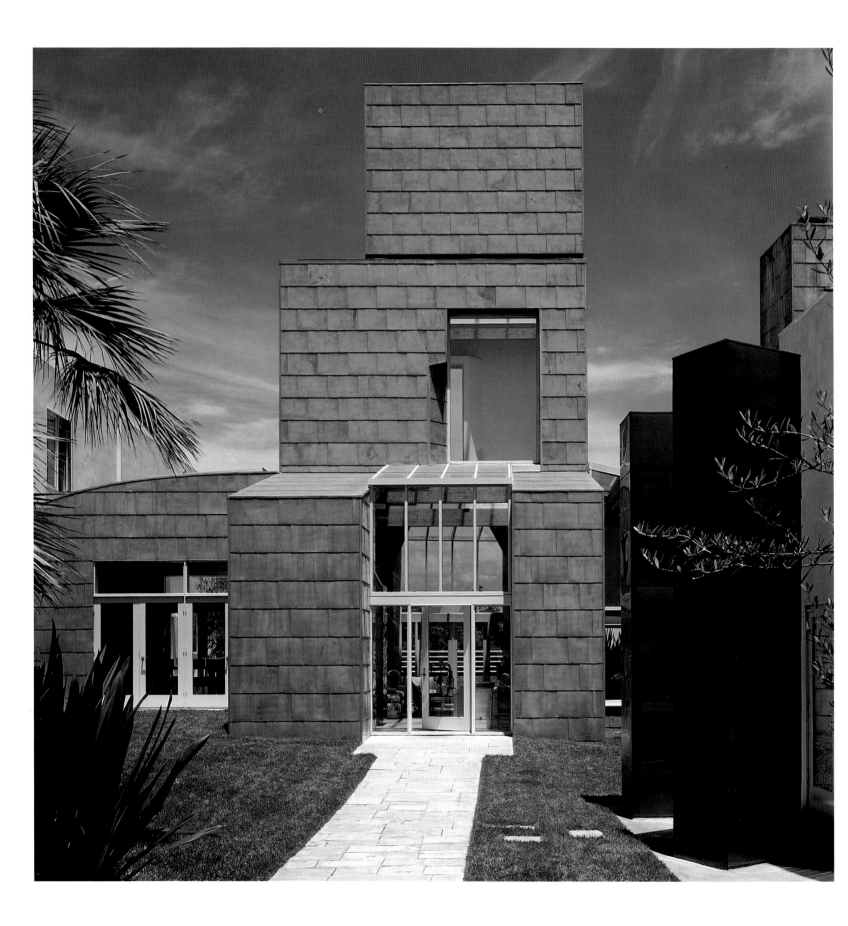

*Frank O. Gehry*

# A house in Brentwood, California

**T**he community of Brentwood, California, which sits astride Sunset Boulevard as it wends its way to the Pacific Ocean, is distinguished from neighboring Bel Air by its lesser ostentation and its more relaxed lifestyle. But incomes are comfortable nonetheless and the population is a mix of young executives and people from the entertainment business. Marilyn Monroe lived here during the last unhappy months of her life.

On a long, narrow strip of land on one of these eucalyptus-lined streets, Frank Gehry has built a house for a diplomat and his family. Gehry's love of fragmentation was given free rein in designing for a family with nearly grown children, who needed some spaces where they could be together and others where each could be alone. Within a surrounding wall of white stucco he laid out, in a functional order, a series of "private boxes."

From the garage and the quarters of the household staff a gallery open on the garden leads to the main building, a tall zinc-covered block that dominates the site and contains a living room, dining room, kitchen and library on the ground floor and the bedrooms of the teenage children one flight up.

*Opposite page*

The house in Brentwood offers the spectacle of varied volumes, strongly contrasted in their shape and material. Here we see the zinc-covered double volume with a box on top, which contains the living room.

The building that holds the master bedroom seems to float on the surface of the pool.

90 A house in Brentwood, California

A stucco-walled unit topped with a brass bulb serves as an office for the head of the household. At one end of the long narrow swimming pool is the private studio apartment for the eldest son, a small structure covered with industrial glass roofing.

As the land sloped strongly toward the rear, Gehry accentuated this by laying out along the slope a series of facilities lined up behind a false arcade, including a gym, sauna and dressing rooms. These lead to a pool from which there emerges a separate building, attached however to the main building by means of the library. This structure, with its brass sheathing and complex geometry, contains the master bedroom. Its position over the water recalls the "free-floating" constructions that Gehry once designed for the Jung Institute. The overall composition of these heterogeneous objects, each one different in shape and color, with their tall chimneys slightly set off from the central core, in some ways resembles an old-fashioned hamlet, or else a micro-cityscape, but it also makes one remember Gehry's fondness for the still lifes of Morandi.

The interior is remarkably understated, tranquil and cozy. Simple furniture stands on waxed parquet floors. Only the fireplace and a large storage unit, both of polished brass, stand out against the white plaster walls. The spectacle is to be found elsewhere: through a variety of carefully-placed openings, which frame a bit of landscape, a patch of sky, a morsel of shrubbery or flowers, or offer a glimpse of blue from the pool or a solitary palm frond overhead. In the master bedroom, on the contrary, the light filters in from above to create an atmosphere of quiet introspection. The huge bed seems to float, suspended between the water of the pool and the firmament. □

White stucco, dark zinc and shiny brass cover oddly-shaped volumes in what almost looks like a random juxtaposition.

Ground plan
1. Garage and gatehouse
2. Covered gallery
3. Dining room
4. Office - 5. Library
6.7. Salons - 8. Fireplace area
9. Guest house - 10. Studio
11. Master bedroom
12. Swimming pool

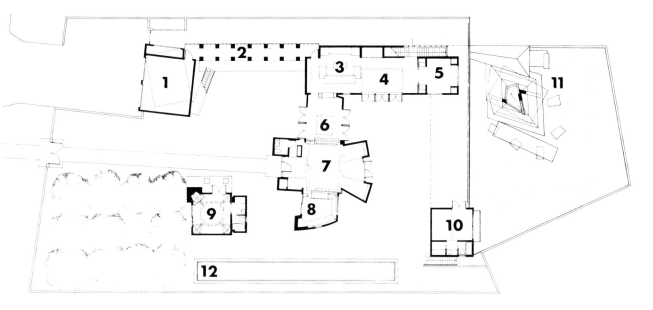

*Above and opposite page*
Views of the grand salon, where light pours in from windows facing the garden as well as from broad skylights above.

The master bedroom, in the building directly on the water.

*Ada Dewes & Sergio Puente*

# A house in San Bernabe, Mexico

Built amid the tall grass on the top of a hill, the home of the architects Dewes and Puente resembles a Toltec temple.

*Opposite page*
An unusual view from the side, this modern version of a "flying buttress."

**S**he is German, he is Mexican. Both architects, Ada Dewes and Sergio Puente are a couple in private as well as in professional life. Ada has lived in Berlin, London, Paris, and Ibiza. Sergio studied at the Architectural Association in London, then in Paris. Both taught at the Universidad Autonoma Metropolitana in Mexico City. Based in the city itself, they have built their house in the outskirts, in the little district of San Bernabe, on a hilltop overlooking the giant metropolis. The house is confidently installed in a form of syncretism, the fruit of their dual background, culture and viewpoint.

First they laid down a Toltec pyramid, an homage to the country's ancient Indian civilizations, on a field of cactuses and desert shrubs in a wilderness surrounded by volcanos. And to carry the metaphor of the temple even further, Dewes and Puente have turned the house to face the sun. The building will feed on sun and run its life on solar time.

The plan of the house is based on a division into two separate concrete blocks joined by an immense glass-covered area, like a sort of patio birdhouse – and a love of birds is present in the spirit of the house. The entrance, on the garden side, is marked by a huge covered staircase. This

staircase serves as the central north-south axis, cutting the structure at right angles. On either side of it are the two small houses within a house, the kitchen and the bathroom. These belong to the first block of the pyramid, the lower part. The street facade belongs to the upper part and contains the apartments. The window in the bedroom roof faces due south.

Inside, where light and shadow play on the wall coverings and furniture, the decoration cultivates references to a more western past. The color scheme is in pale nuances of pearl gray and straw yellow. The materials are noble – wood and marble, mirrors and ceramics. The overall effect is refined and feminine, with a touch of nostalgia.

Seen from the garden, the front gate and broad staircase open the house to the sunlight. In the dazzling light, rhythmic contrast is provided by the black tiles, stilts and grillwork.

*Opposite page*
On the opposite side of the house, the terrace faces Mexico City.

Under the staircase is
the living room, in
tones of gray and black.
A spare look, with
some fine pieces of Art
Deco furniture. A
grouping of rattan
chairs and a well-worn
leather armchair add a
few intimate touches.

The temple of Dewes and Puente obeys the whims of light, while the pyramidal base provides its weightiness. Its situation on an exact north-south axis confirms the sense of ritual of these two adepts of nature. Here, far from the haunts of men and their harmful ways, they live in harmony with heaven and earth.

The inner setting, by contrast, is lighter, more sentimental. There is no hi-tech, but some Art Deco furniture pays homage to the genius of time past, a past which, in this cactus-rimmed hermitage, seems all the more distant. □

The bathroom, situated
in one of the two
independent blocks at
the entrance to the
pyramid. Fairly small in
size, it is embellished
by a covering of marble
and a mirror assembled
of diamond-shaped
sections, for a rather
1930s effect.

*Opposite page*
The bedroom under the
eaves, with a door
opening onto the
terrace and a large
window, through which
light pours in directly
over the bed. The
dressmaker's model is
nicknamed "Venus."

In the entrance, a
strange still life made
up of wooden
cylinders, sectioned
mirrors and a pair of
well-worn boots.

*Eric O. Moss*

# A house in Los Angeles, California

Built in a residential quarter of Los Angeles, this house bears a strong resemblance to a fortress. The varied forms of the windows, the unusual placement of the front door (tucked away in a corner), and the beams jutting out of the roof, form an architecture of lines in movement, both outside, as here on the south facade, and inside as well, where most of the space is taken up by a vast kitchen/dining room/living room.

**T**he Lawson-Westen House is all built around a kitchen. If, as they say, the American kitchen in its time had the effect of a revolution, then this one makes an impact like a tornado. In his way, the architect has expressed the desire of his clients to make this room the nerve center of the house, a setting not only for culinary pleasures but also for convivial interaction which, if we are to judge by the architecture, is bound to be as flavorful as it is unusual...

The kitchen occupies a circular space on the ground floor. It is open both on the living room and dining room, around which are areas reserved for cupboards and storage space. Above the sink and the vast work surface of veined marble rise a astonishing assortment of ascending lines, straight or curved, broken or spiral. This is the staircase, imprisoned like

In a severe tone and
defensive mode, the
side facing the street
expresses the same
extremely dynamic
qualities.

*Opposite page*
View downward on the
kitchen from the
stairwell, which is
crossed by a
passageway leading to
the bedrooms.

6/20/89

Sketches by
Eric Moss of the work
in progress

*Opposite page*
The vast living room
soares three levels
high, with a wonderful
spatial interpenetration,
fine workmanship and
choice of materials. The
architect's humorous
touch is seen in the
shape of the windows.

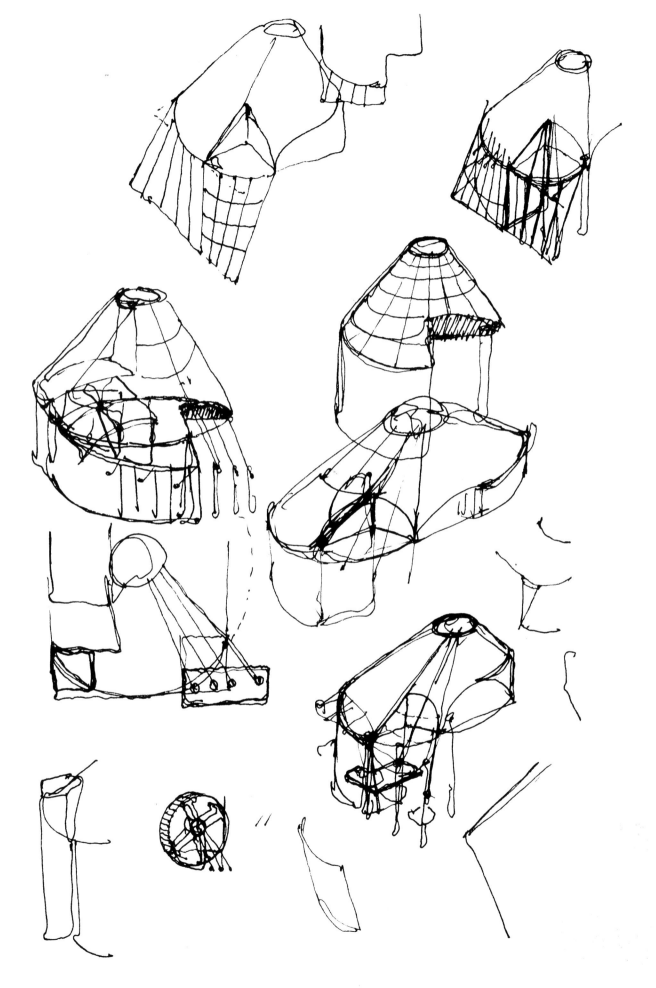

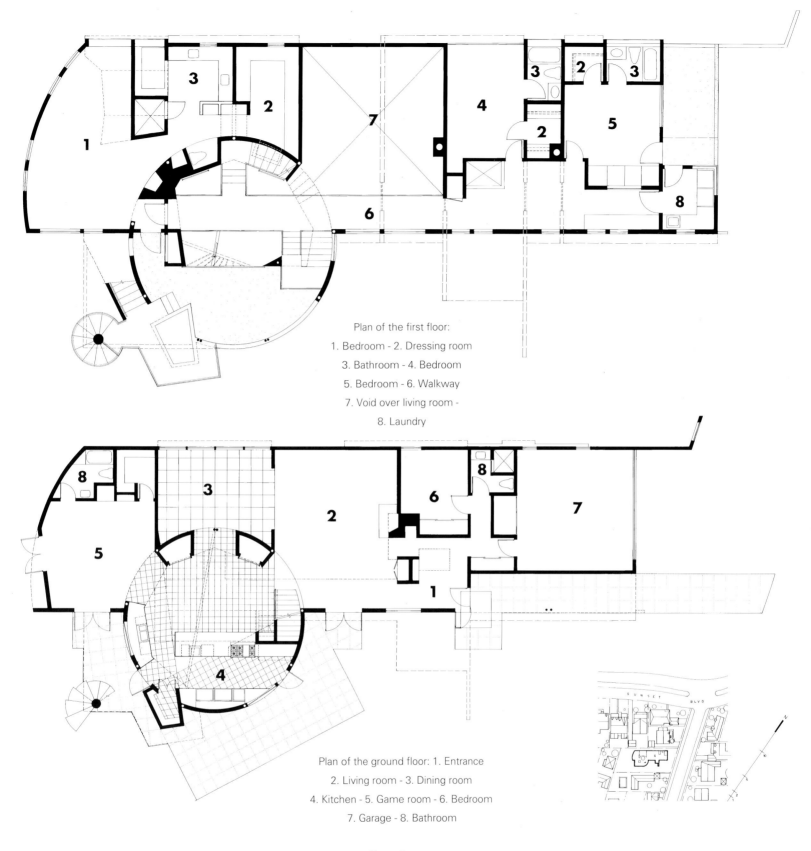

Plan of the first floor:

1. Bedroom - 2. Dressing room

3. Bathroom - 4. Bedroom

5. Bedroom - 6. Walkway

7. Void over living room -

8. Laundry

Plan of the ground floor: 1. Entrance

2. Living room - 3. Dining room

4. Kitchen - 5. Game room - 6. Bedroom

7. Garage - 8. Bathroom

*Opposite page*

The living room seen from the kitchen
sink. The shades of orange and metallic
blue contrast and complement one
another, while the design of the fireplace
finds its echo in the visible beams and
staircase railings.

Under a conical roof,
the main bedroom
occupies an
asymmetrical space.
Fresh spring colors
enter through the
windows, enhancing
the wooden furniture
designed by the
architect himself.

some wild beast in a cylindrical cage, whose walls can barely contain its overpowering energy. Metal girders, supporting pillars and fragments of the circular structure jut out of the walls to form a monumental sculpture. Elsewhere, high above the living room, wood and metal combine to give the appearance of a mended beam joined together by some clever artisan. Eric Moss likes to try his hand at metalwork, at times using shapes from another age, like the window with its pointed arch that clearly resembles that of a cathedral. An incongruous touch, but not a meaningless one. It is like a remnant of an earlier stage of the project, a memory of the dialogue between the architect and his client. In the same way, the street facade on the east side bears the dramatic movement of a roof that looks as if it hasn't been completed yet: cut and twisted masses, split, tilted surfaces and bared beams.

Some five meters high, a walkway flung over open space leads to the children's rooms on one side, the parents' on the other. After this risky-looking passage, the atmosphere on arrival is a peaceful one. A wooden bed offers its inviting curves. A long strip cut out of the roof exposes the ceiling laths and lets daylight in. At night it is a Jacob's ladder to the land of dreams. As for the windows, Eric Moss multiplies, declines and conjugates the concept beyond the wildest dreams of any standard grammar of architecture: sash windows, gothic windows, folded, slanted, broken or abstract windows or simply square windows of different sizes and alignments. Doors, beams and stairways get the same treatment: removed from their traditional contexts and proportions, they take on the role of a constant questioning. The front door, for example, situated at a corner on the west of the building, reflects the paradox of a dual desire for transparency and security.

Located in a prosperous quarter of Los Angeles, the Lawson-Westen House turns its fortresslike frontage to the street, complete with armored door and barred windows. The concrete outer shell affirms the same solidity. On the side facing the garden the same concrete is used for the tower and its off-center roof. The monumental quality is thereby accentuated, but the fortress in not unbreachable. A spiral stairway climbs outside to the terrace, cut out of an oblique side of the cone, then continues upward to the summit, from which one can contemplate the Pacific Ocean. □

*John Keenen & Terence Riley*

# A "water mill" in Lambertville, New Jersey

In the 18th-century the English landscape architect William Kent (1684-1748) created little "temples" in his gardens, modest architectural jewels without frills, set down in greenery at the water's edge, the whole rimmed by forests, like a landscape painted by Claude Lorrain. In those days, the Palladian style came in to offset the taste for the baroque. This was followed by a somewhat formal neo-Grecian revival style, exemplified in the United States by Thomas Jefferson.

Temples, pavilions, summer-houses... each period had its word to evoke the ideal hermitage and to honor the spirit of the garden. Thus, when asked to built a "casino", that is, a little "casa" on a wooded hillside in New Jersey, the architects John Keenen and Terence Riley opted for a discreet reference to history, a muted love affair with the past.. It would have been hard to do otherwise. For here in Lambertville, New Jersey, in the south of Hunterdon County on the banks of the Delaware River, the whole region is steeped in American history. The pre-revolutionary past is everywhere, the 18th-century cannot be ignored.

The "water mill" by Keenen and Riley, front and rear views. All the "restructuring" signs have been deliberately left visible. The drystone walls of the old mill hold the main part of the house, while the brand new addition contains the kitchenette and utilities. It is topped by a completely distinct, completely transparent structure that forms a belvedere and terrace.

Stone, metal and glass
are juxtaposed for a
startling effect. The
approach is a tongue-in-
cheek, almost
subversive, reference to
history.
This staircase is the only
access to the belvedere.

*Opposite page*
In the upper part the
architects have purposely
used every motif to give
a feeling of lightness:
grids, trellises, thin
planks, stilts and a cage
of glass. The marked
contrast makes the old
stone walls look even
heavier and more
opaque.

Close-up showing the
point of juncture
between the old stone
wall and the new glass
cage.

*Opposite page*
Inside the old mill, the
walls have been
surmounted with a
band of glass that runs
around the entire room.
The original doors and
windows have been
respected, so that the
room remains blissfully
cool on warm summer
nights.

Keenen and Riley built the "casino" requested by their clients on the ruins of an 18th-century water mill, surrounded by tall acacia trees and at some distance from the main house of a holiday estate. The owners wanted to be able to receive guests here, to have dinners, relax and enjoy themselves in company. Also to sleep on hot summer nights.

The terrain is on a slope, with the swimming pool at the lower end. The plan was determined by the old mill. The architects did not touch the old stones – the masonry of their thick walls is perfect just as it is. They also respected the original windows and doors. They merely added a sort of appendix on the western flank of what would become the main room. This would hold the kitchenette and the bathroom. This new addition supports a flight of steps that lead upstairs to the terrace and belvedere – a glass cage, completely covered yet completely transparent. The supports on which it stands, along with the metal trellis, form a grid and give the structure both its unity and its graceful appearance.

Stone and glass. Strength and fragility. The two structures, though superimposed, do not communicate. Their materials are sharply contrasted, their functions separated, their uses different. One is a sheltered haven, the other an open space. One is cool, the other bathed in light. From these oppositions (or complementarities) results a perfectly-finished little jewel of a country house. They might have chosen to ignore the mill, or to restore it. Now, integrated into the project, it is no longer an old ruin, nor is it a mere token of authenticity. It is a reasoned link between past and present, between work and leisure and between a vernacular peasant architecture and the architecture, erudite but understated, of the university. □

John Keenen & Terence Riley 117

*Bart Prince*

# A house in Corona del Mar, California

This astonishing house, built at the edge of the Pacific Ocean, is an extraordinary mixture of organic forms and images from science fiction. Beside the undulating lines of wood are sharply structured volumes with acute angles and straight lines.

**B**art Prince designed this home in Corona del Mar, south of Los Angeles, for Joe Price. The house, which follows the shape of the small promontory on which it stands, looks out on the Pacific Ocean. Seen from the road, it looks rather like a beached whale washed up on a rock amid the pines. The only openings are the prism-shaped windows tucked away in the folds of its skin. This "skin", made of slim wooden slats, contains part of the house. Like some supple organic tissue, it stretches toward the ocean, then opens up to liberate a series of circular structures like a string of living cells.

At the heart of this construction, deployed in the form of a huge arc, is a curved swimming pool lying in a black granite garden and rimmed with a scattering of rocks. A clump of bamboo and a slightly arched bridge over the water suggest some affinities with Japan. A passage amid the pebbles leads to a sunken space, the tea-house. In some places the rock on which the house is built peeps out from the tiled floor; an artificial river flows among monumental pillars surrounded by columns and serving to support the circular capsules. Each pillar opens out to become an umbrella – its spokes reinforced by brass corners, the whole

The wooden covering that shimmers in the light gives way, on the ocean side, to a series of circular structures, the "capsules." Made of wood and brass, they form a complex facade extended by a terrace.

The wood is worked
with a fine
craftsmanship worthy
of Gaudí.

*Opposite page*
On the ground floor,
the various areas are
laid out in a circular
arrangement around
the swimming pool.

Plan of the ground floor
1. Living room
2. Open air terrace
3. Kitchen/Dining room
4. Bedroom
5. Bathroom
6. Swimming pool
7. Entrance

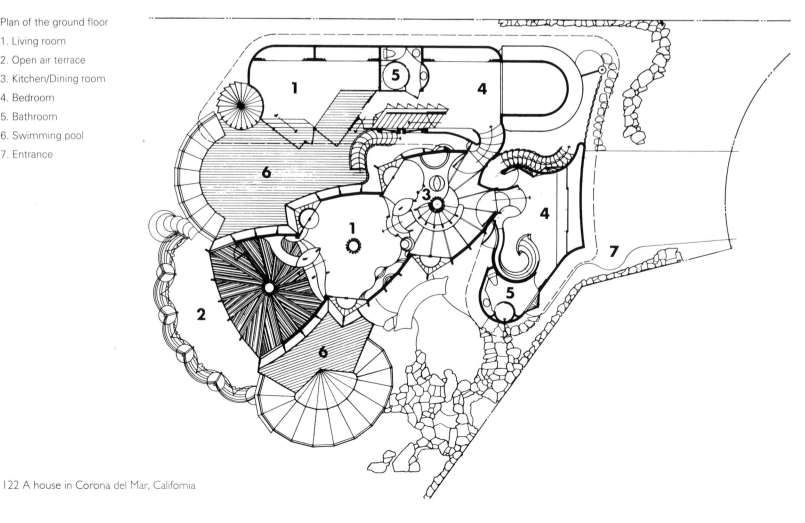

thing forming a sort of tent. This marriage of styles, part Japanese, part flamboyant Gothic, revised and amended by the fertile imagination of Bart Prince, creates a universe that is strange and unsettling.

For one thing, the entrances are hard to find. In this house the notions of inside and outside are not at all clearly differentiated, the forms and materials are often identical. Wood or metal may simulate in one place the wall of a cave, elsewhere the skin of a reptile. A dark corner may conceal a corridor that leads to the master bedroom, the living room or the kitchen. These three spaces, which share most of the ground floor, form a three-lobed facade toward the ocean. At one end is the kitchen, which manages to combine a dome borrowed from religious architecture, armchairs like those in a company boardroom and a table that looks like it belongs in a sushi bar.

Staircases wind here and there around pillars and lead to one of the capsules that form the upper floor: these hold the children's bedrooms, the television room and a workshop. Topped with brass, their lower part covered by a wooden shell, these capsules extend onto a vast terrace surrounded by a railing that seems to come straight from a merry-go-round. Inside, lacquered wood, carpeting and windows of brightly-colored glass create a medley of shapes, vines and plumed birds form an artificial jungle where movement in a straight line is all but impossible.

In this house, the inner space is an unstable mixture that develops like an organic entity. It grows and determines the exterior, generating forms linked together without a break from deep in the heart of the house to the natural environment outside. □

The teahouse: a universe of baroque forms in the which the curve dominates. The water flows between the monumental pillars that support the capsules and a narrow, sinuous staircase rises between wood-covered walls.

126 A house in Corona del Mar, California

The combined effect is
dense and heavy, with
dark corners and an
atmosphere of tropical
humidity.

The kitchen is a large hemisphere with an imposing round table at its center, the whole room lit from above through the ample glass dome.

*Opposite page*
In one of the capsules, Bart Prince's fertile imagination gives rise to motifs that seem to spring from a sci-fi film set.

# A house in Glencoe, Illinois

Built in the form of a zigzag to incorporate the old oak trees, this house is only a short distance from Lake Michigan.

*Opposite page*
This living room and its extension into an open air terrace offer their wallspace for collecting contemporary art. Here, no new artwork would be unthinkable.

**A**n interplay of large squares takes up the full frontal section of this inclined facade. French windows divided into different size rectangles, a bow-shaped door with three asymmetrical bars and a multitude of "unpaired" dormer windows in varied and irregular shapes offer up triangles, trapezoids, circles and half moons. This house is definitely an eye-opener – or is it a series of eyes? Sometimes they look generously over the landscape, other times with a gaze that is almost suspicious, like the menacing look of a bull's-eye window. The house flirts and invites us to look inside.

Designed for a connoisseur of contemporary art by the architects Laurinda Spear and Bernardo Fort-Brescia from Arquitectonica the project was completed in 1988. Set on a remarkable site dominating lake Michigan from some 20 meters (60 feet), the house is part of a relaxed upscale suburb along the lake's western shore, north of Chicago.

The house was built in the shape of a "Z" to avoid cutting down any of the old oak trees standing in the meadow. In order to accommodate the owner's passion for collecting contemporary art, the living room and its terrace provide ample wall space and room for new acquisitions. Another requirement was to incorporate a full-scale workout area

The villa's inclined front facade entirely made up of windows. The "oversize" roof provides shelter from the elements.

*Opposite page*
This is a playful entranceway: a stage-like doorstep, a jagged and mirrored guardrail, windows of all shapes and sizes. Outwardly poking fun at convention, the architects have instilled this villa with a relaxed air.

within the villa. The result is a 20 meters (60 feet) swimming pool and a mini gym complete with all the equipment for body building. And lastly a flat "overhanging" roof gives shade and protection from the wind.

But along with comfort, Laurinda Spear and Bernardo Fort-Brescia have given equal attention to the villa's finishing touches, to its materials and colors: pink or light gray granite walls; black, white or green marble; bright maple wood parquet. The paintings on the walls add the final touch...

Accustomed to creating bold and unique designs, the architects have, nevertheless, spared this luxurious villa from nouveau-riche stereotypes. The villa does not fall into the trap of resembling an art gallery thanks largely to its rhythmic, open facade, and even to its insolence and its "gadgetry." Far from openly advertising itself as a place for art, its controlled asymmetry and "lopsided geometry" puts things back in their place – in their rightful place. □

The bow-shaped front door crowned
with circular windows. To the right, an
artwork signed Gilbert and George.

*Opposite page*
Above, the inclined facade makes for a
low-angle view, accentuating the sense
of overlooking the lake from on high.
Below, the swimming pool and the
lively touch of its jagged windows.

*Jeanne McCallum*

# A house in San Diego, California

Behind a facade that resembles a traditional adobe house, a series of intricately overlapping volumes are laid out around a central courtyard.

**T**his house, built in a residential quarter of San Diego, is situated, just like its region of southern California, near the Mexican border, at a crossroads of styles and cultures.

The project proposed to the architect Jeanne McCallum was to add an extension, intended as a studio/workshop, to an existing building, a simple house in the traditional adobe style that stood at the southern edge of its property.

McCallum's plan integrated the original building into a larger complex of which it became one of the sections, the whole ensemble oriented in such a way as to create a courtyard centered around the cool shade of a tree. The entrance, with its wooden door and the facade of the studio that extends from it, give the place a visual resemblance to a ranch. In the courtyard, however, a surprise awaits the visitor. The workshop consists of three overlapping volumes laid out along the western edge of the land. On the other side a wooden terrace, raised above ground level, prolongs the former building toward the courtyard.

The first volume is parallel to the western boundary and opens on the south with a composite facade: the concrete

Plan

A. Old house

1. Living room

2. Dining room

3. Kitchen

4. Bedroom

5. Bathroom

6. Terrace

7. Access path

B. New building

8. Workshop

9. Study

10. Terrace

11. Passageway

12. Staircase to
bedroom

13. Boundary of
bedroom

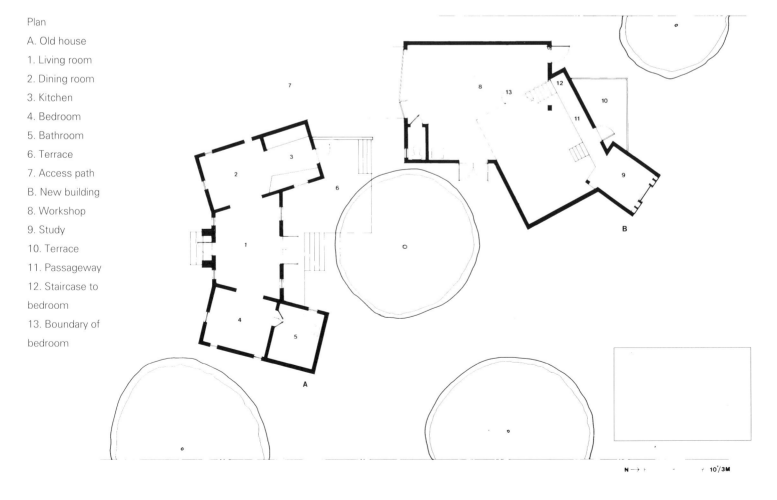

The complex juxtaposition of forms creates differences in level and a fragmentation of the facade that reveals a pronounced taste for eclecticism.

Inside the house, a rustic atmosphere prevails. The space is fragmented but the use of wood as the sole material provides a feeling of unity. The architect's fondness for oblique lines and cut-off edges is visible.

wall has a wooden garage door, and over that a triangular window that brings light to the upper floor occupied by the bedroom. The other two cubes are set at angles to overlap each other, thus creating a dynamic feel both outside and in. Inside the house, the different spaces are linked by cascades of staircases.

The last addition, on the north side, is a volume posed several meters above ground on a small wooden terrace. Unlike the rest of the buildings, whose walls are made of brightly-colored stucco, this structure is covered with corrugated metal. This differentiation of facades creates a combination of planes, with a rhythm given by the colors, the oblique lines of the roofs, the patterns of the beams. All the areas have large windows, oriented to receive only northern light, except for the bedroom, which also has an eastern exposure.

Door and window frames, beams and exposed pillars convey an intelligible image of the internal structure. A single space fills the three volumes, fragmented into clearly differentiated zones yet without partitions. Wood, the traditional material of the American southwest, is omnipresent, and gives the interior a feeling of warmth and simplicity: bare bulbs, exposed hinges and windows extending to the midpoint of the walls are references to old-fashioned artists' studios. The world of the western is there too, in the form of the traditional rocking chair. By all these allusions, the architect blends rustic and modern into a composite style inspired by both Hispanic and American trends. □

*Peter Forbes*

# A house in Marion, Massachusetts

Whether covered in snow or battered by the wind, this maritime house holds forth with a certain detachment. Its great resistance to the elements seems to lift it out of history. Its architectural strength lies in its symmetry, its eccentricity in its roof, its sobriety in its materials of shingles, bricks and concrete.

*Opposite page*
One of the two rotundas on either side of the house.

*Following pages*
The side and the facade with the terrace facing the sea.

**T**he barrenness of New England's coast, with its windy shores, sharp spits and gentle beaches, coves, estuaries and coastal pines has always attracted Peter Forbes. It is no surprise that his designs dot its entire length.

Dividing his time between Boston and Southwest Harbor, Maine, Forbes is especially drawn to the wilder stretches of this coast where his houses turn toward the sea with a certain restraint and calm.

Marion, Massachusetts, is tucked behind the hook of Cape Cod. Built on an exceptional site, the house sits on a hill lined with pines dominating Buzzard's Bay, a bay with deep waters, protected from the ocean by the Elisabeth Islands and the Barnstable peninsula. A little further down on the same bank is the town of New Bedford and a few hundred yards inland the beginning of a canal connecting the bay to Cape Cod. As one would expect, people are good sailors here, the owner of the house being no exception. This villa in Marion is clearly designed to appeal to a sailor; the house has a special roof for checking the weather or for hanging sails out to dry. Its focal point is this square tower, topped by a viewing post, reminiscent of 18th and 19th-century New England houses. From the roof one used to be

A full side view with
the bay in the
background.

*Opposite page*
The facade facing the
garden with its roof
extension like an
awning over the
colonnade entrance
porch.
The home stands out
for its perfect
symmetry and
geometry.

able to spot ships or clippers heading for the harbor. The rest
of the layout is perfectly symmetrical with two almost
identical wings, each one ending in a circular balcony.

Protecting the front facade is a porch roof supported by
four columns, while on the back, the facade opens out onto
a terrace. The tower, unlike the rest of the house, has three
levels with a square room at the very top that commands
views of the entire bay. From here one can access the
ramparts through a trap door. The living room, dining room
and kitchen share the first floor and the bedrooms with their
respective bathrooms take up the full length of the second.

The windows, distributed vertically or horizontally, along
with the columns and the double chimney create a well
studied geometry. More opulent and self-contained than the
house on Great Cranberry, Maine, this villa nevertheless
shares the same sober materials: shingled walls and roofs in
white wood, aluminum window frames, piles, retaining walls
and chimneys built in concrete bricks.

Not a flourish or whim comes to interrupt Forbes's
designs; his houses have no need to flaunt their charm.
Rather, Forbes lets the landscape dominate. It is the
landscape that woos the onlooker; it alone indulges in
sudden outbursts. The house in Marion, like all this East
Coast architect's creations, chooses sobriety. This is perhaps
the Boston heritage we think of as Puritanism, having
something of the restraint, the pride of the first settlers. □

The sitting, as seen above from the staircase, opens out onto a terrace overlooking the bay.

*Opposite page*
The stairs rising up the tower where a little room on the third floor commands an all-around view.

*Agustín Hernández*

# A house in Mexico City, Mexico

This extraordinary concrete and steel protrusion – the "house" built by Agustín Hernández – flaunts the entanglement of residential houses below. In terraces down the slope, at the foot of its 35 meters (100 feet) thick double wall, is a swimming pool and garden.

**A** boat on dry-dock? A spaceship anchored in an urban landscape? A piece of a crane sticking out from the decor or an exercise in the geometry of solids? Or is this just the folly of an engineer or a draughtsman? No, this is a "house," a house that flouts the void, anchored to the hillside with its head in the clouds. "In the valley of Mexico City, man feels suspended between earth and sky, he oscillates between opposite forces and powers," wrote the late poet Octavio Paz in the *Labyrinth of Solitude*. Not without arrogance, this strange-looking object, ostentatious in its originality, implies a certain mood, a refuge between inwardness and pride. Architecturally, however, it could be considered as a transposed form of "Mexicanness." Again, in the words of Octavio Paz, "the preeminence of the closed over the open does not only manifest itself as indifference and mistrust [...] but also as the love of Form."

From the outset of the project, the terrain posed a serious constraint – a 20 meters (60 feet) drop at a 65° angle. To make the most of this topography, architect Agustín Hernández decided on a bold and daring approach.

The top of the hill has a panoramic view over the Bosque de Guanabanos, one of Mexico City's many residential

A solution pushed to the extreme or the prowess of an engineer... The house is like a steel cockpit suspended in the circular opening of two concrete blocks. The zoom effect over the landscape is astonishing.

*Opposite page*
On top of the hill, the two upper "wings" of the prism on the street side.

The living room and kitchen share the same level; the main bedroom and Jacuzzi are upstairs. The lower part holds two bedrooms and their bathrooms.

suburbs, while the foot of the hill gets lost in a mesh of non-descript houses topped by their ever present parabolic antennas. A double 35 meters (100 feet) concrete wall raises the "house" vertically so that its main entry is level with the street. As if held by a clamp, the skeleton is like a steel prism, attached to the round openings crowning each retaining wall. Supported in two places, the framework is attached to the entrance level facing the street and integrated into the cross section at a distance of 2,30 meters (7 feet). Four triangular "wings" bolted to the metal beams provide the volume, adding verticality and symmetry to the whole like two inverted twin figures. The entrance is equally monumental.

The house comprises five levels with the living room, kitchen and bathroom on the main street level, forming the heart of the structure. A step above is the main bedroom with a Jacuzzi and below, set in the inverted pyramid, are two bedrooms and their respective bathrooms. The lower gallery serves as a storage space and wine cellar.

Whether spaceship or tunnel, the immense skylight that runs along the entire length of the structure only increases the impression of a corridor while filters, portholes, loopholes and skylights diffract the sunlight, bringing a warm violet light to rest on the concrete and steel.

Perched some thirty meters above the ground, Agustín Hernández's "house," expresses its fondness for form and its aim to dominate a dull, uniform neighborhood. With its condescending gaze, however, it establishes a clearly hierarchical relationship with its surroundings, responding more to a feudal than an aerial calling, as though from its height, in the never-ending quest for clean air in Mexico City, the "house" could gain by just hanging in the sky... □

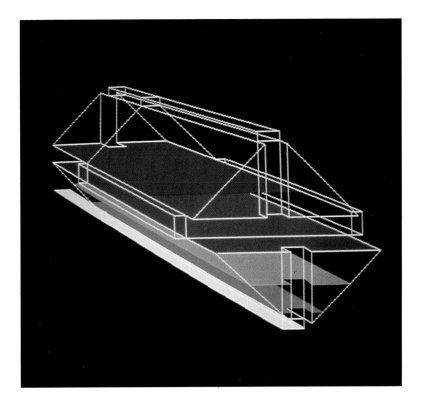

A computer-generated diagram of the volume.

*Opposite page*
The stairs cascade down from the swimming pool to the base of the supporting walls. The rear of the property is no less astonishing or cunning than the rest.

The wine cellar in the "gallery."

*Opposite page*
The main bedroom in the top of the prism and the living room in the center. To accommodate the low ceilings, a Japanese-style decor makes for living closer to the floor.

# Biographies

## ANDERSON & SCHWARTZ ARCHITECTS

### ANDERSON Ross S.

Born in San Francisco in 1951.
Graduated from Stanford University (1973) and Harvard.
Partner of MLTV & Turnbull Associates.
Opened his agency with Schwartz in New York in 1984.

### SCHWARTZ Frederic

Born in New York in 1951.
Director of the New York branch Venturi, Scott-Brown & Associates until 1984.

**Agency works:** offices of Windham Hill Productions (1985), offices and show-room of Isaac Mizrahi, New York (1990), Napa House, Napa Valley, California (1990).

## ARQUITECTONICA

### SPEAR Laurinda

Born in Rochester, Minnesota, in 1950 .
Graduated from Columbia (1975) and M.I.T.
Partnership with her husband, Bernardo Fort-Brescia, in agency founded in Miami (1977).

### FORT-BRESCIA Bernardo

Born in Lima, Peru, in 1951.
Graduated from Princeton (1973) and Harvard (1975).

**Agency works:** in Miami, Spear house (1976-1978), The Palace (1979-1982), The Atlantis (1980-1982), North Dade Justice Center (1984-1987) ; in Lima, Mulder house (1983-1985), Banco de Credito (1983-1988) ; Center for Innovative Technology, Herndon, Virginia (1985-1988).

## ADA DEWES & SERGIO PUENTE

### DEWES Ada

Born in Germany in 1944.
Graduated from Hanover Werkkunstschule. Studied painting at Fine Arts Academy, Berlin, then linguistics in Mexico City (1973-1977).
Doctorate from École des hautes études en sciences sociales, Paris (1973).
Since 1975, teaches at School of Arts and Sciences, Universidad Autonoma Metrolopolitana, Mexico City.

### PUENTE Sergio

Born in Mexico City, 1942.
Graduate of the Architectural Association School of Architects, London (1970).
Doctorate from École des hautes études en sciences sociales, Paris (1982).
Since 1975, teaches at School of Arts and Sciences, Universidad Autonoma Metrolopolitana and, since 1980, at the Center for Demographic and Urban Studies, Mexico City

### FORBES Peter

Worked for Skidmore, Owings & Merrill, Chicago (1965-1966), then partner of PARD Team Inc. Architects and Planners, Boston.
President of Forbes Hailey Jeas Esneman (1972-1980).
In 1980 founded Peter Forbes & Associates in Boston and Southwest Harbor, Maine.
Visiting professor at Harvard (1989, 1991, 1994), and University of Michigan (1987).
Has earned over 30 awards (among them the Record House Award 1989).

**Recent works:** Southwest Harbor library (1988-1989), church in Sacco, Maine (1990), shops for Origins Natural Resources, many homes including his own on Mount Desert Island (1991-1993).

### GEHRY Frank O.

Born in Toronto, Canada, 1929.
Graduated from University of Southern California in 1954.
Founded Frank O. Gehry Associates in 1962. FAIA 1974.
Lives and works in Los Angeles.
Has taught at University of Southern California, U.C.L.A., Yale and Harvard.
Pritzker Prize 1989.

**Major works:** Ron Davis studio, Malibu (1970-1972), Hollywood Bowl (1970-1982), Santa Monica Place (1973-1980), headquarters of Rouse Company, Columbia (1974), Gehry house, Santa Monica (1979-1987), California Aerospace Museum, Los Angeles (1982-1984), Wosk Residence, Beverly Hills (1982), Norton house, Venice (1983), Winton Guest House, Wayzata, Minnesota (1984-1986), Schnabel house, Brentwood (1986), restaurant Fish Dance, Kobe, Japan (1986-1989), Walt Disney Concert Hall, Los Angeles (1989), Vitra Museum, Weil am Rhein, Germany (1989), Art Museum, University of Minnesota (1990), Guggenheim Museum, Bilbao, Spain, 1997.

### HERNÁNDEZ Agustin

Graduated from Escuela Nacional de Arquitectura, University of Mexico City (ENA), in 1954.
Taught at ENA from 1957 to 1968.
Vice-president of Mexican Academy of Architects (1979-1980).

**Works:** in Mexico City, Escuela de Ballet Folklorico (1968), home of Amalia Hernandez (1970), Military School (1975), Hospital unit IMSS (1975), "Bosques de las Lomas" house (1988); in Cuernavaca, Meditation Center (1986).

### ISOZAKI Arata

Born at Oita, Kyushu Island, Japan, 1931.
Graduated from Architecture School, Tokyo (1954).

Founded his agency in 1963.
Gold medal of RIBA in 1986.

**Main projects:** in Japan, Modern Art Museum, Gunma (1971-1974), Tsukuba Center (1978-1983), Musashi golf club-house (1987), Mito ArtTower (1986-1990), small museum Nagi MoCA, Nagi-cho, Okayama (1992-1994), B-con Plaza, Oita (1991-1995), Concert Hall, Kyoto (1992-1995); in the USA, Museum of Contemporary Art, Los Angeles (1981-1986), Disney Team Building, Orlando, Florida (1990-1994).

### ISRAEL Franklin D.

Born in New York, 1945, died in 1997.
Studied at University of Pennsylvania, Yale and Columbia.
Prix de Rome for architecture (1973).
Worked with Giovanni Pasanella in New York and Llewelyn-Davies, Weeks, Forestier-Walker in London and Teheran.
Art director for Paramount Pictures (1978-1979). Took part in film projects.
Opened his agency in 1983.

**Works:** offices for Propaganda Films, Hollywood and Virgin Records, Beverly Hills; house for Robert Altman in Malibu, Goldberg-Bean Residence (1991), Art Pavilion, Beverly Hills (1991), Woo Fong Pavilion, Silver Lake (1992).

### JONES Fay

Graduated from University of Arkansas (1950) and Rice (1951).
Started out working with Frank Lloyd Wright.
Taught at University of Oklahoma , then Arkansas (1966-1974).
Tucker Prize, 1981 and 1982. Gold Medal of American Institute of Architects

**Major works:** Thorncrown (chapel 1981), house at Hogeye (1987), Pinecote pavilion (1990).

### KAPPE Ray

Graduated from University of California (1951).
Member of American Institute of Architects (AIA) since 1953.
From 1953 to 1968 worked on 40 residential and 8 commercial projects.
Founded agency as partnership, Kahn Kappe Lotery Boccato, renamed Kappe Architects Planners in 1981.
Since the 1980s has been exploring the question of energy.
In 1972 founded and managed (until 1987) SCI-ARC, Southern California Institute of Architecture.
Neutra Award (1987). Topaz Medal (1990) for excellence in educational action, awarded by AIA and ACSA.
Maybeck Award (1995). Gold Medal (1996) from Los Angeles AIA.

**City planning projects:** design for new town in Valencia, urban renewal plans for city centers of Inglewood, Compton, Santa Monica and Watts-Willowbrook, promenade and parking area for Charmlee Park/Santa Monica Mountains, low rent apartment complex (255 apartments) in Pasadena.

## JOHN KEENEN & TERENCE RILEY

### KEENEN John

Studied history at Georgetown University and architecture at Columbia.
Before opening his own agency, worked for several New York firms and the International Rescue Committee (IRC) in Thailand.
Has taught since 1986 at the New York Institute of Technology.

### RILEY Terence

Graduate of University of Notre-Dame and Columbia.
Partnership with John Keenen since 1984.

## KRUECK & SEXTON ARCHITECTS

### KRUECK Ronald

Graduated from Illinois Institute of Technology, Chicago (1970).
Studied painting at Art Institute of Chicago (1976-1978).
Worked for C. F. Murphy Associates (1970-1971), then Hammond Bebey Associates (1971-1976).
In 1978, with Olsen, created agency Krueck & Olsen. (Olsen replaced by Sexton in 1991).
Assistant professor (1975-1983) then professor (since 1992) of architecture at Illinois Institute of Technology.
Member of American Institute of Architects, Chicago Chapter.
National Honor Award (1986) and Honor Award (1996) of AIA Chapter Chicago.

### SEXTON Mark

Graduated from Illinois Institute of Technology (1980).
Worked at Skidmore Owings & Merrill (1978), then at Danforth Rockwell Carow (1979-1980).
In 1980, joined Krueck & Olsen, senior partner with Krueck in 1991.
Member of American Institute of Architects, Chicago Chapter.

**Major works of agency:** in Chicago, A Steel and Glass House (1981), showroom The Thonet (1982), The Painted Apartment (1983), Runnion residence (1985), apartments Untitled N°1 (1987) and N°2 (1988), Stone Residence (1988), Lee Hill offices and Peck residence (1990), Cochrane residence and The Stainless Steel Apartment (1992), Herman Miller showrooms and Silverman residence (1993), A Brick and Glass House (1996); in Lincolnshire, Illinois headquarters of Hewitt Associates (1988), and its Center for the Eastern Region, Rowayton, Connecticut (1989); in Los Angeles, offices of Northern Trust Company of California (1993); in Newport Beach, Northern Trust Company of California Bank.

## McCALLUM Jeanne

Born in Detroit in 1957.
Graduated from University of Auburn (1980).
Created agency MODA (McCallum Ostendorf Design Associates), in 1985, in San Diego.

**Works:** in San Diego, Weiss/Churchill residence (1993) and studio/workshop for Robert Treat (1995).

## MOSS Eric Owen

Born in Los Angeles in 1943.
Studied at Berkeley and Harvard (1972).
Opened his agency in 1973.
Professor and managing member of Southern California Institute for Architecture. Has taught at Yale, Harvard, Copenhagen and Vienna.
Member of American Institute of Architecture. Has won over 30 awards, AIA and "Progressive Architecture".

**Major projects:** Central Housing Office, University of California at Irvine, (1986-1989); in Culver City, Lindblade Tower, Paramount Laundry (1987-1989), Gary Group (1988-1990), Tne Box (1990-1994), IRS Building (1993-1994); Samitaur Building and PS Building in Los Angeles.

## PREDOCK Antoine

Graduated from Columbia University (1962).
Founded his agency in 1967. Based in Albuquerque, New Mexico.
Member of American Institute of Architects (1981).
Visiting Critic at Harvard University in 1987. Visiting Professor and Visiting Critic at Southern California Institute of Architecture in 1984, 1990, 1995 and 1996.
Winner of numerous prizes including Record Houses 1970, 1972, 1977, 1982, 1986, 1990 and 1994, and AIA California Council Merit & Honor in 1990, 1996 and 1997.

Major works:
**Residences:** in California, Venice Residence, Venice and Rosenthal at Manhattan Beach, (1989) ; Fuller residence, Desert Highlands (1987) and Zuber residence, Paradise Valley, Arizona (1989); Turtle Creek house, Dallas, Texas (1988)...
**Recent works:** American Heritage Center and Art Museum, University of Wyoming, Laramee, Wyoming (1987), Arizona Science Center in Phoenix, Arizona (1991), Museum of Science & Industry, Tampa, Florida (1991), Hispanic Cultural Center of New Mexico, Albuquerque (1993), Spencer Theater, Ruidoso, New Mexico (1994), Teaching Museum and art gallery of Skidmore College, Saratoga Springs, New York (1996).

## PRINCE Bart

Born in Albuquerque, New Mexico, in 1947.

Assistant to Bruce Goff (1968-1973).
Opened his agency in 1973.
Assisted Bruce Goff on Japanese Art Pavilion project, Los Angeles County Museum of Art, and completed the building after Goff's death.

**Works:** villas Bart Prince in Albuquerque (1984), Joe Price at Corona del Mar, California (1989), Henry Whiting in Sun Valley, Idaho (1991), houses Mead/Penhall (1992-1993) and High Residence, Mendocino County, California.

# Bibliography

## General bibliography

*American Houses Now. Contemporary Architectural Design,* Thames & Hudson, London, 1997.
*American Masterworks. The Twentieth Century House,* Rizzoli, New York, 1995.
*Amérique latine. Architecture 1965-1990,* by Jorge Francisco Liernur, Electa, Milan, 1990.
*México :Nueva Arquitectura,* by Antonio Toca/anibal Figueroa, GG, Mexico City/Barcelona, 1991.
*Modern American Houses,* Harry N. Abrams Inc./Architectural Record, New York, 1992.
*New American Architects,* vol III, Benedikt Taschen, Cologne, 1997.

## Monographs

*Antoine Predock Architect,* Rizzoli, New York, 1994.
*Antoine Predock,* Global Architecture n°52, A.D.A., Tokyo, 1997.
*Arata Isozaki : Architecture 1969-1990,* The Museum of Contemporary Art, Los Angeles, Rizzoli, New York, 1991.
*Arata Isozaki,* Global Architecture, A.D.A., Tokyo, 1991.
*Eric Owen Moss : Buildings and projects 1,* Rizzoli, New York, 1991.
*Eric Owen Moss : Buildings and projects 2 (1991-1995),* Rizzoli, New York, 1996.
*Krueck & Sexton,* The Monacelli Press, New York, 1997.

# Photo credits

Pages 54 to 61, front cover and back cover : photos Korab Hedrich Blessing
Pages 26 to 33 : photos Reiner Blunck
Pages 102 to 111 : photos Tom Bonner
Pages 44 to 53, 62 to 69, 94 to 101, 150 to 157 : photos Richard Bryant/Arcaid
Pages 88 to 93 : photos Marc Darley
Pages 6, 136 to 141 : photos David Heawitt/Anne Garrison
Pages 112 to 117 : photos Eduard Hueber
Pages 34 to 43, 70 to 79, 130 to 135, 142 to 149 : photos Timothy Hursley
Pages 8 to 15 : photos Michael Moran
Pages 16 to 25, 80 to 87, 118 to 129 : photos Alain Weintraub

Printed and bound in Great Britain by
Butler & Tanner Ltd, Frome and London